This book is presented to:

Parker

On the occasion of:

your baptism

From:

Grandma & Gramps

This book is for my nephew, John Francis Fagundes.
–Anthony DeStefano

Dedicated to Allison and Ryan
With much love,
Dad

–Richard Cowdrey

The Sheep That No One Could Find

Text copyright © 2014 by Anthony DeStefano
Artwork copyright © 2014 by Richard Cowdrey

Published by Harvest House Publishers
Eugene, Oregon 97402
www.harvesthousepublishers.com

ISBN 978-0-7369-5611-6

For more information about Anthony DeStefano, please visit his website: www.anthonydestefano.com

Design and production by Mary pat Design, Westport, Connecticut

All Scripture quotations are taken from the Holy Bible, New International Version®, NIV®. Copyright © 1973, 1978, 1984, 2011, by Biblica, Inc.™ Used by permission of Zondervan. All rights reserved worldwide. www.zondervan.com

Printed in China.

16 17 18 19 20 21 /LP/10 9 8 7 6 5 4 3

The Sheep That No One Could Find

Anthony DeStefano
Illustrated by Richard Cowdrey

HARVEST HOUSE PUBLISHERS
EUGENE, OREGON

There was once a Good Shepherd
Who tended His sheep
In a field by a mountain,
High, green, and steep.

The sheep would go grazing
Right down to the sea.
They always were happy
And always were free.

As long as they followed
The Shepherd they knew,
Nothing could harm them
Or frighten them too.

3

But one of the sheep
Decided one day
The words of the Shepherd
Were hard to obey.

Instead he decided
To do things HIS way.
He even decided
To run far away.

So he snuck off alone
As fast as he could,
Over a river
And into a wood.

4

"At last," said the sheep
As he stood near a tree,
"I won't have to follow
The Shepherd and be
Like all of the others—
I'll really be free!"

5

So into the valley,
The little sheep crossed
And wandered all day
Until he was lost.

Lost and confused,
He wasn't aware
A hungry old wolf
Had spotted him there.

The wolf licked his lips
And drooled at the sight.
He got an idea
And said with delight,
"I think I'll have lamb chops
For dinner tonight!"

But in order to take
The sheep by surprise,
The wolf had to use
A most clever disguise.

8

He put on a sheep suit,
A mask on his head,
Then waved to the sheep
And cheerfully said,

"How about having
Some dinner with me?
I live over there—
Would you like to come see?"

The sheep, who felt lonely,
Said in reply,
"I'd love to have dinner—
Just you and I."

But when they arrived
At the hungry wolf's lair,
There wasn't a trace
Of food anywhere.

The wolf grinned and said,
"There is no mistake.
You see, silly sheep,
I'm just a big fake!

"Now come over here.
Don't try to go back.
YOU are my dinner,
My tasty sheep snack!"

The little sheep screamed
And dived underneath
The wolf's snapping jaws
And razor-sharp teeth.

11

He raced through the forest,
Past buzzards and bees.
The wolf chased behind
But got lost in the trees.

p into the mountain,
he frightened sheep flew.
e had no idea
st what he would do.

ut all of a sudden,
e came to a stop
he moment he got
o the high mountaintop.

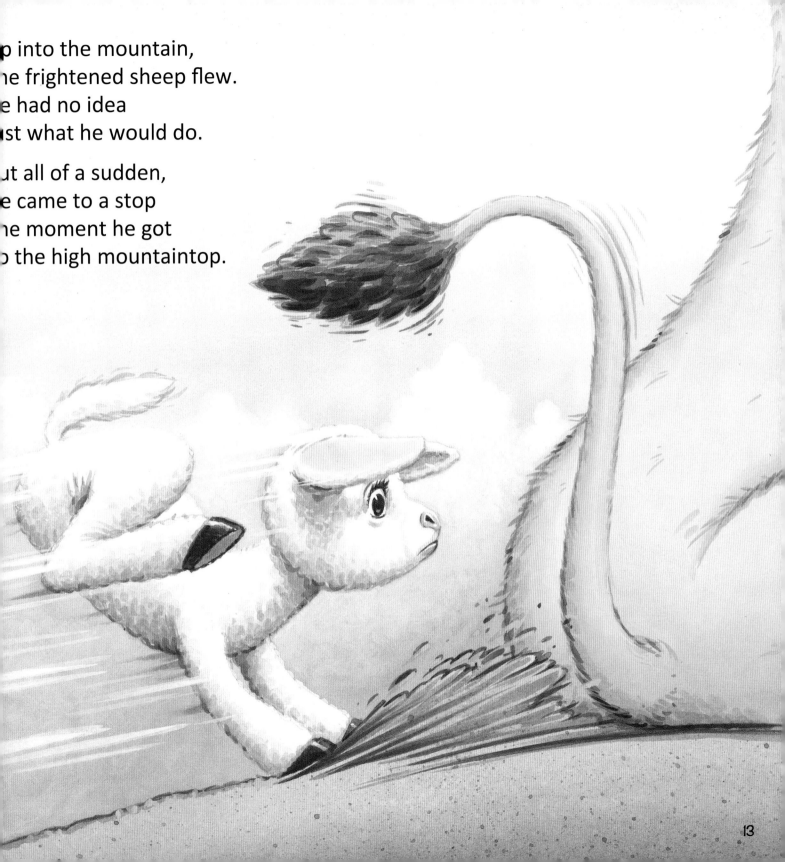

For blocking his path,
The little sheep saw
A huge, angry lion
Who started to ROAR!

The lion was mean
And prideful and bad.
He prowled through the country
And always was mad.

In order to show off
His strength and his might,
He tried to devour
All the sheep in his sight.

With fury he growled,
"How dare you come here!
This is MY mountain!
 Isn't that clear?"

Then making a lunge
With his powerful paws,
He sliced at the air
With his long, deadly claws.

The sheep backed away
On the mountain's flat top
But couldn't go further
Or down he would drop.

So he leaped on the lion
And slid down his tail.
He landed behind him
Then ran down the trail.

Far off in the distance,
He saw a tall tree.
"Finally," he said,
"A safe place for me."

He climbed up the tree,
And taking a chance,
He crawled to the end
Of a thin, leafy branch.

"At last," breathed the sheep,
"I'll take a short rest.
And just like a bird,
I'll hide in a nest."

But the sheep felt so sad.
"I want to go home.
I'm tired of being
So scared and alone.

"I miss the Good Shepherd.
I'd much rather be
Following Him
Than stuck up this tree!"

But just at that moment
From out of nowhere,
A slithering snake
Hung down in the air.

The snake was a liar—
an evil one too.
The words that he spoke
Were always untrue.

20

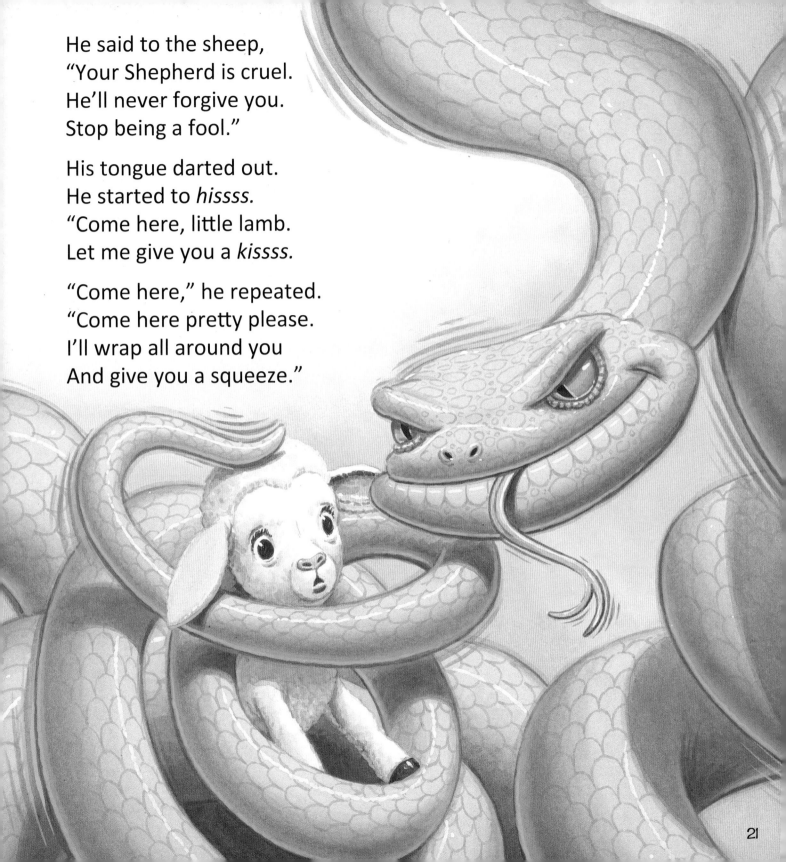

He said to the sheep,
"Your Shepherd is cruel.
He'll never forgive you.
Stop being a fool."

His tongue darted out.
He started to *hissss.*
"Come here, little lamb.
Let me give you a *kissss.*

"Come here," he repeated.
"Come here pretty please.
I'll wrap all around you
And give you a squeeze."

21

The sheep wiggled out.
He barely got free.
He jumped to the ground
And started to flee.

The snake was behind,
The little sheep knew.
The wolf and the lion
Were chasing him too!

23

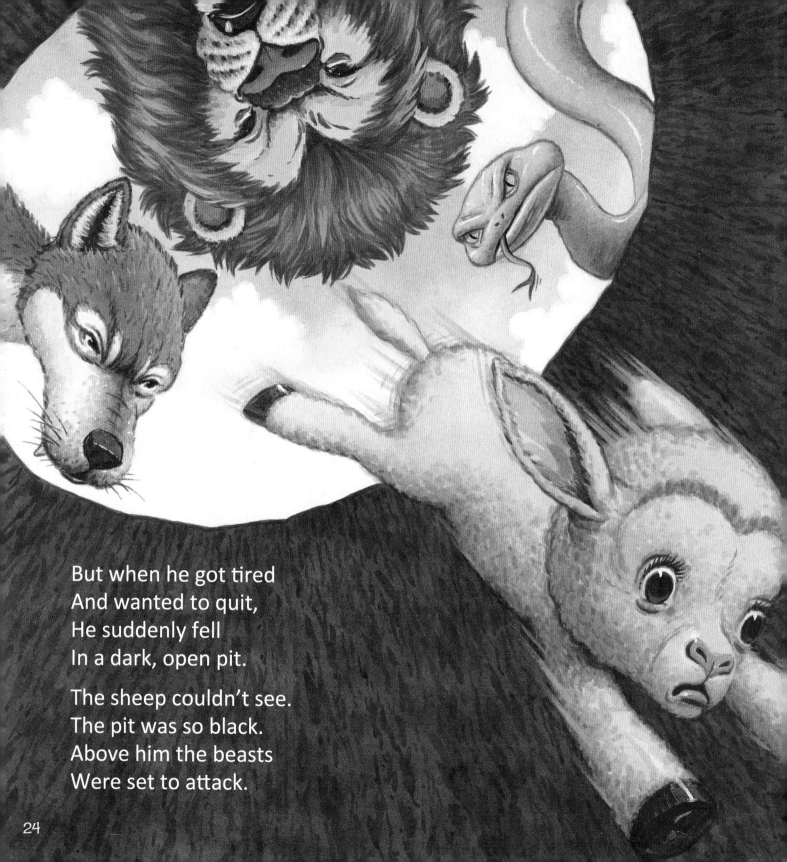

But when he got tired
And wanted to quit,
He suddenly fell
In a dark, open pit.

The sheep couldn't see.
The pit was so black.
Above him the beasts
Were set to attack.

"Oh, what can I do?"
The little sheep sighed.
"I'm trapped and alone
And just want to cry.

I've been so confused,
So wrong, and so blind.
My Shepherd was caring
And loving and kind.

I should never have left.
It was all a mistake.
I'm tired of wolves
And of lions and snakes."

But then the sheep heard
A most wonderful sound.
It came from above—
From up on the ground.

The Shepherd was back!
The Shepherd was here!
The Shepherd was calling
His name loud and clear!

He had left all His flock
For one sheep who was lost—
To rescue and save him
No matter the cost.

He trounced the huge lion.
He crushed the sly snake.
He flung the old wolf
By his tail in a lake.

Then He pulled the sheep out
From down in the pit,
And on His strong shoulders,
He made the sheep sit.

He carried him back
With a smile that was bright
To the field by the mountain—
What a beautiful sight!

The sheep were all glad
To see their small friend.
He promised to never
Leave them again.

To the Shepherd he said,
"I'm sorry I strayed.
Forgive me for all
The mistakes that I made."

"All is forgiven,"
The Shepherd replied.
And the sheep could detect
Tears of joy in His eyes.

"My heart is so happy.
My love is so deep.
Welcome back to your family.
Welcome *home,* My lost sheep."

Then Jesus told them this parable:
"Suppose one of you has a hundred sheep and loses one of them. Doesn't he leave the ninety-nine in the open country and go after the lost sheep until he finds it? And when he finds it, he joyfully puts it on his shoulders and goes home… I tell you that in the same way there will be more rejoicing in heaven over one sinner who repents than over ninety-nine righteous persons who do not need to repent."

Luke 15:3-7

[Jesus said,] "I am the good shepherd."

John 10:11